Rabbit

Pooh

SMUDGE

WOL

eOR

BLOT

This book belongs to:

Name *MaxMM*

Address *160*

☎

A A MILNE
THE
POOH
ADDRESS BOOK

ILLUSTRATED by E.H.SHEPARD

Methuen Children's Books

First published in 1984
by Methuen Children's Books
Michelin House, 81 Fulham Road, London SW3 6RB
Reprinted 1984 (twice), 1987, 1988, 1989 and 1990

Typeset, printed and bound in Great Britain by
BPCC Hazell Books
Aylesbury, Bucks, England
Member of BPCC Ltd.

ISBN 0 416 49290 8

"What's this that I'm looking at?"
said Eeyore still looking at it.
    "An A," said Rabbit,
"but not a very good one."

Name _____

Address _____

_____

☎ _____

A

Name

Address

☎

Name

Address

☎

Name

Address

☎

A

Name

Address

☎

Name

Address

☎

Name

Address

☎

A

Name

Address

☎

Name

Address

☎

Name

Address

☎

A

Name

Address

☎

Name

Address

☎

Name

Address

☎

A

Name

Address

☎

Name

Address

☎

Name

Address

☎

A

Name _____

Address _____

_____

☎ _____

Name _____

Address _____

_____

☎ _____

Name _____

Address _____

_____

☎ _____

Pooh

A Bear of Very Little Brain.

Name _____

Address _____

_____

_____ ☎ _____

Name _____

Address _____

_____

_____ ☎ _____

B

Name

Address

☎

Name

Address

☎

Name

Address

☎

B

Name

Address

☎

Name

Address

☎

Name

Address

☎

B

Name _____

Address _____

_____

☎ _____

Name _____

Address _____

_____

☎ _____

Name _____

Address _____

_____

☎ _____

B

Name _____

Address _____

_____

☎ _____

Name _____

Address _____

_____

☎ _____

Name _____

Address _____

_____

☎ _____

B

Name

Address

☎

Name

Address

☎

Name

Address

☎

Name _____ $\mathbb{B}$

Address _____

_____

_____ ☎ _____

Name _____

Address _____

_____

_____ ☎ _____

Name _____

Address _____

_____

_____ ☎ _____

Cottleston, Cottleston, Cottleston Pie.
A fly can't bird, but a bird can fly.
Ask me a riddle and I reply:
"Cottleston, Cottleston, Cottleston Pie."

Name

Address

☎

C

Name

Address

☎

Name

Address

☎

Name

Address

☎

C

Name

Address

☎

Name

Address

☎

Name

Address

☎

C

Name

Address

☎

Name

Address

☎

Name

Address

☎

C

Name _____

Address _____

_____

☎ _____

Name _____

Address _____

_____

☎ _____

Name _____

Address _____

_____

☎ _____

C

Name

Address

☎

Name

Address

☎

Name

Address

☎

C

Name

Address

☎

Name

Address

☎

Name

Address

☎

The Piglet was sitting on the ground
at the door of his house blowing happily
at a dandelion, and wondering whether
it would be this year, next year, sometime,
or never.

Name _____

Address _____

_____

☎ _____

D

Name

Address

☎

Name

Address

☎

Name

Address

☎

D

Name

Address

☎

Name

Address

☎

Name

Address

☎

D

Name

Address

☎

Name

Address

☎

Name

Address

☎

D

Name

Address

☎

Name

Address

☎

Name

Address

☎

D

Name

Address

☎

Name

Address

☎

Name

Address

☎

Name

Address

☎

Name

Address

☎

Name

Address

☎

D

"Yes, Eeyore,"
said Piglet,
sniffing a little.
"Here it is. With –
with many happy returns
of the day."
And he gave
Eeyore the small
piece of damp rag.

Name _____

Address _____

_____

☎

_____

E

Name

Address

☎

Name

Address

☎

Name

Address

☎

E

Name

Address

☎

Name

Address

☎

Name

Address

☎

Name

Address

☎

Name

Address

☎

Name

Address

☎

E

Name

Address

☎

Name

Address

☎

Name

Address

☎

E

Name

Address

☎

Name

Address

☎

Name

Address

☎

E

Name

Address

☎

Name

Address

☎

Name

Address

☎

Once upon a time, a very long time ago now, about last Friday, Winnie-the-Pooh lived in a forest all by himself under the name of Sanders.

Name _____

Address _____

_____

☎ _____

F

Name

Address

☎

Name

Address

☎

Name

Address

☎

Name _____ $\mathbb{F}$

Address _____

_____

☎ _____

Name _____

Address _____

_____

☎ _____

Name _____

Address _____

_____

☎ _____

. . . they could see the whole world
spread out until it reached the sky,
and whatever there was all the world over
was with them in Galleons Lap.

G

Name

Address

☏

Name

Address

☎

Name

Address

☎

Name

Address

☎

G

Name _____

Address _____

_____

_____ ☎ _____

Name _____

Address _____

_____

_____ ☎ _____

Name _____

Address _____

_____

_____ ☎ _____

G

Name

Address

☎

Name

Address

☎

Name

Address

☎

G

Name

Address

☏

Name

Address

☏

Name

Address

☏

Name

Address

☎

Name

Address

☎

Name

Address

☎

G

Name

Address

☎

Name

Address

☎

Name

Address

☎

"Hallo, Rabbit.
Fourteen, wasn't it?"

"What was?"

"My pots of honey what I was counting."

Name _____

Address _____

_____

☎

H

Name

Address

☎

Name

Address

☎

Name

Address

☎

H

Name

Address

☎

Name

Address

☎

Name

Address

☎

I

I AM SCERCHING FOR A NEW HOUSE
FOR OWL SO HAD YOU RABBIT.

Name _____

Address _____

_____

☎

I

Name

Address

☎

Name

Address

☎

Name

Address

☎

Name

Address

☎

Name

Address

☎

Name

Address

☎

J

But he didn't feel very brave,
for the word which was really jiggeting
about in his brain was "Heffalumps".

What was a Heffalump like?

Name

Address

☎

J

Name

Address

☎

Name

Address

☎

Name

Address

☎

J

Name

Address

☎

Name

Address

☎

Name

Address

☎

J

Name

Address

☎

Name

Address

☎

Name

Address

☎

J

Name

Address

☎

Name

Address

☎

Name

Address

☎

J

Name

Address

☎

Name

Address

☎

Name

Address

☎

J

Name

Address

☎

Name

Address

☎

Name

Address

☎

Now it happened
that Kanga had felt
rather motherly
that morning,
and Wanting to Count Things.

Name _____

Address _____

_____

☎ _____

K

Name

Address

☎

Name

Address

☎

Name

Address

☎

Name

Address

☎

Name

Address

☎

Name

Address

☎

"A lick of honey,"
murmured Bear to himself,
"or – or not, as the case
may be." And he
gave a deep sigh,
and tried very hard
to listen to what
Owl was
saying.

Name

Address

☎

L

Name

Address

☎

Name

Address

☎

Name

Address

☎

L

Name

Address

☎

Name

Address

☎

Name

Address

☎

"Notice
a meeting of everybody
will meet at the House at Pooh Corner
to pass a Rissolution
By Order
Keep to the Left Signed Rabbit."

Name

Address

☏

M

Name

Address

☎

Name

Address

☎

Name

Address

☎

M

Name

Address

☎

Name

Address

☎

Name

Address

☎

M

Name

Address

☎

Name

Address

☎

Name

Address

☎

M

Name

Address

☎

Name

Address

☎

Name

Address

☎

M

Name _____

Address _____

_____

☎ _____

Name _____

Address _____

_____

☎ _____

Name _____

Address _____

_____

☎ _____

M

Name

Address

☎

Name

Address

☎

Name

Address

☎

NorTH PoLE
DICSoVERED By
PooH
PooH FouND IT

Name _____

Address _____

_____

☎

N

Name

Address

☎

Name

Address

☎

Name

Address

☎

N

Name

Address

☎

Name

Address

☎

Name

Address

☎

PLEZ CNOKE
IF AN RNSR
IS NOT REQID

"He's found a name for it,"
said Christopher Robin,
lazily nibbling
at a piece of grass,
"so now all he wants
is the house."

Name _____

Address _____

_____

☎ _____

O

Name

Address

☎

Name

Address

☎

Name

Address

☎

Name

Address

☎

Name

Address

☎

Name

Address

☎

"Rise, Sir Pooh de Bear,
most faithful of all my Knights."

Name _____

Address _____

_____

☎

_____

P

Name

Address

☎

Name

Address

☎

Name

Address

☎

P

Name

Address

☎

Name

Address

☎

Name

Address

☎

And, as I say, you never can tell with bees.
The important bee to deceive is the Queen Bee.

Name

Address

☎

Name

Address

☎

Name

Address

☎

Name

Address

☎

Name

Address

☎

Name

Address

☎

Name

Address

☎

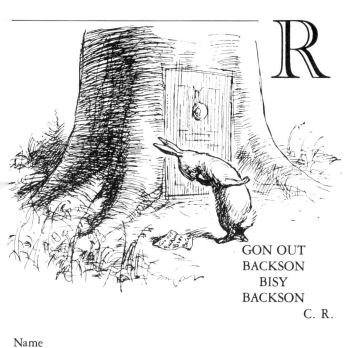

R

GON OUT
BACKSON
BISY
BACKSON

C. R.

Name _____

Address _____

_____

☏ _____

R

Name

Address

☎

Name

Address

☎

Name

Address

☎

R

Name

Address

☎

Name

Address

☎

Name

Address

☎

"It's Small!" cried Piglet.

"Oh, *that's* who it is, is it?" said Pooh.

Name _____

Address _____

_____

☏ _____

S

Name

Address

☎

Name

Address

☎

Name

Address

☎

S

Name

Address

☎

Name

Address

☎

Name

Address

☎

S

Name

Address

☏

Name

Address

☏

Name

Address

☏

Name _____ $\mathbb{S}$

Address _____

_____

_____ ☎ _____

Name _____

Address _____

_____

_____ ☎ _____

Name _____

Address _____

_____

_____ ☎ _____

S

Name

Address

☎

Name

Address

☎

Name

Address

☎

S

Name

Address

☎

Name

Address

☎

Name

Address

☎

T

"Tiggers don't like honey."

Name

Address

☎

T

Name

Address

☎

Name

Address

☎

Name

Address

☎

T

Name _____

Address _____

_____

☎ _____

Name _____

Address _____

_____

☎ _____

Name _____

Address _____

_____

☎ _____

T

Name

Address

☎

Name

Address

☎

Name

Address

☎

T

Name _____

Address _____

_____

☎ _____

Name _____

Address _____

_____

☎ _____

Name _____

Address _____

_____

☎ _____

T

Name

Address

☎

Name

Address

☎

Name

Address

☎

T

Name

Address

☎

Name

Address

☎

Name

Address

☎

"It is because you are
a very small animal
that you will be Useful
in the adventure before us."

Name
_____

Address
_____

_____

☎
_____

U

Name

Address

☎

Name

Address

☎

Name

Address

☎

U

Name

Address

☎

Name

Address

☎

Name

Address

☎

. . . and if you save us all,
it will be a Very Grand Thing
to talk about afterwards.

Name _____

Address _____

_____

 _____

Name

Address

☎

Name

Address

☎

Name

Address

☎

Name

Address

☏

Name

Address

☏

Name

Address

☏

V

"Tracks," said Piglet.
"Paw-marks."

He gave a little
squeak of
excitement.
"Oh, Pooh!
Do you think it's a – a – a Woozle?"

Name
_____

Address
_____

_____

☎
_____

Name

Address

☎

Name

Address

☎

Name

Address

☎

W

Name

Address

☎

Name

Address

☎

Name

Address

☎

"It's a little AnXious," he said to himself,
"to be a Very Small Animal
Entirely Surrounded by Water."

Name _____

Address _____

_____

☎ _____

Name _____

Address _____

_____

_____ ☎ _____

Name _____

Address _____

_____

_____ ☎ _____

Name _____

Address _____

_____

_____ ☎ _____

X

Name

Address

☎

Name

Address

☎

Name

Address

☎

"I'm planting a haycorn, Pooh,
so that it can grow up into
an oak-tree, and have lots
of haycorns just outside the
front door
instead of
having to
walk miles
and miles,
do you see, Pooh?"

Name

_____

Address

_____

_____

☎

Name

Address

☎

Name

Address

☎

Name

Address

☎

Y

Name

Address

☎

Name

Address

☎

Name

Address

☎

Isn't it funny
How a bear likes honey?
Buzz! Buzz! Buzz!
I wonder why he does?

Name

Address

Z

Name

Address

☎

Name

Address

☎

Name

Address

☎

Name

Z

Address

☎

Name

Address

☎

Name

Address

☎

My friends' birthdays:

_____

_____

_____

_____

_____

_____

_____

_____

_____

_____

_____

Rabbit.

Kanga.

Pooh.

SMUDGE

WOL

eOR

BLOT